W9-BRX-785

My Hands and Feet

Brian Enslow

Bailey Books
an imprint of
Enslow Publishers, Inc.
40 Industrial Road
Box 398
Berkeley Heights, NJ 07922
USA
http://www.enslow.com

Bailey Books, an imprint of Enslow Publishers, Inc.

Library of Congress Cataloging-in-Publication Data

Enslow, Brian.
My hands and feet / Brian Enslow.
p. cm. — (All about my body)
Summary: "Simple text and photographs present a story about hands and feet"
—Provided by publisher.
Includes bibliographical references and index.
ISBN 978-0-7660-3816-5 (alk. paper)
1. Hand—Juvenile literature. 2. Foot—Juvenile literature. I. Title.
QM548.E57 2011
612.97—dc22

2010014877

Paperback ISBN: 978-1-59845-173-3

Printed in he United States of America

052010 Lake Book Manufacturing, Inc., Melrose Park, IL

10 9 8 7 6 5 4 3 2 1

To Our Readers: We have done our best to make sure all Internet Addresses in this book were active and appropriate when we went to press. However, the author and the publisher have no control over and assume no liability for the material available on those Internet sites or on other Web sites they may link to. Any comments or suggestions can be sent by e-mail to comments@enslow.com or to the address on the back cover.

♻ Enslow Publishers, Inc., is committed to printing our books on recycled paper. The paper in every book contains 10% to 30% post-consumer waste (PCW). The cover board on the outside of each book contains 100% PCW. Our goal is to do our part to help young people and the environment too!

Photo Credits: Shutterstock.com.

Cover Illustration: Shutterstock.com.

Note to Parents and Teachers

Help pre-readers get a jumpstart on reading. These lively stories introduce simple concepts with repetition of words and short simple sentences. Photos and illustrations fill the pages with color and effectively enhance the text. Free Educator Guides are available for this series at www.enslow.com. Search for the *All About My Body* series name.

Contents

Words to Know

kick

swim

wings

These are hands.

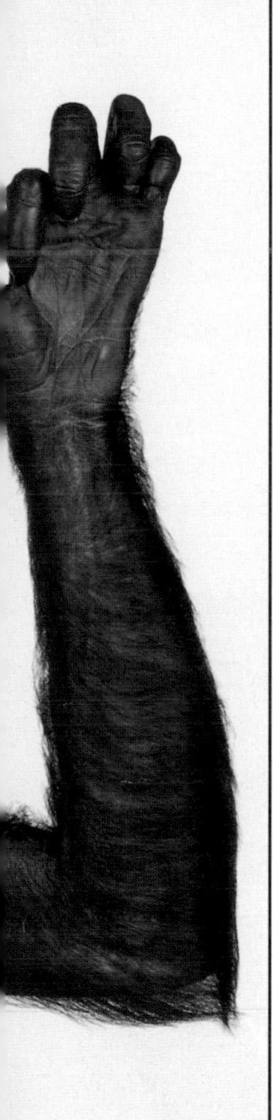

Big hands. Are these your hands?

Fish fins.
Are these your hands?

Bird wings.
Are these hands?

These are feet.

Four feet.
Are these your feet?

Funny feet.
Are these your feet?

Swim feet.
Are these your feet?

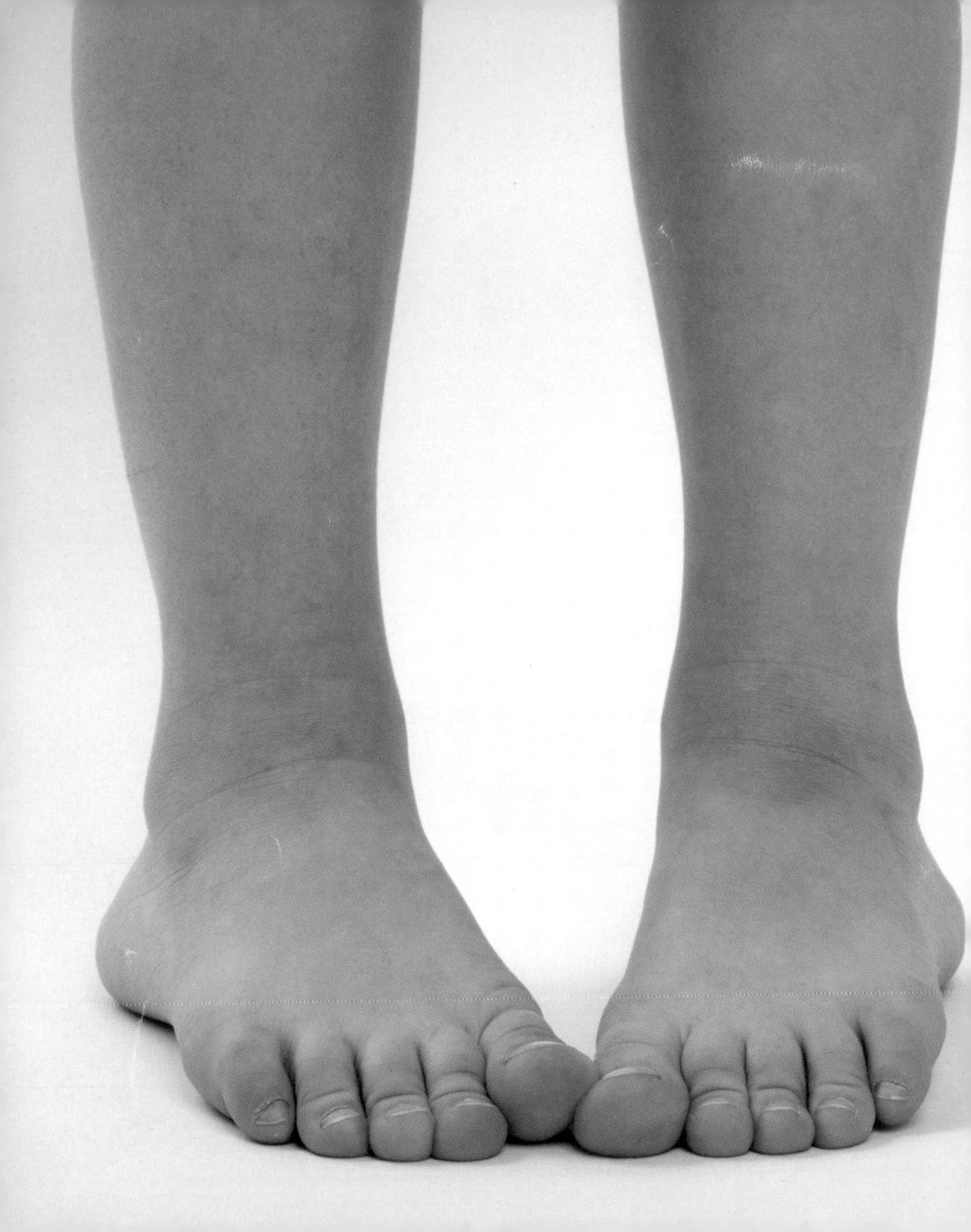

Kid feet.
Are these your feet?

Your hands and feet?

My hands and feet.

Read More

DeGezelle, Terri. *Taking Care of My Hands and Feet.* Mankato, Minn.: Capstone Press, 2006.

Klingel, Cynthia Fitterer. *Feet/Los Pies*. Strongsville, OH: Gareth Stevens Publishing, 2010.

Web Sites

Enchanted Learning
<http://www.enchantedlearning.com/dictionarysubjects/body.shtml>

Sid Says on PBS Kids
<http://pbskids.org/sid/#/sidSays>

Index

Guided Reading Level: B
Guided Reading Leveling System is based on the guidelines recommended by Fountas and Pinnell.

Word Count: 53